GOD

OF THE

KITCHEN

JON TRIBBLE

GLASS LYRE PRESS

Cover art: Najjar Abdul-Musawwir
Author photo: Allison Joseph
Design & layout: Steven Asmussen
Copyediting: Linda E. Kim

Glass Lyre Press, LLC
P.O. Box 2693
Glenview, IL 60025
www.GlassLyrePress.com

ACKNOWLEDGMENTS

Acknowledgment is made to the following publications for poems that originally appeared in them or are forthcoming.

The Account: "In the Hall of the Mountain King" and "Risen"

Atticus Review: "Chicken Dance," "Famous Hot Gravy," "God of the Kitchen," "Livers and Gizzards," and "Wings of Skin"

The Blue Mountain Review: "Full Thickness," "Honest Labor," "Honey on My Tongue," "Insecticide: The Four-Way Test," and "This Day the Lord"

North American Review: "The King Is Dead"

Pirene's Fountain Literary Journal: "How Not to Get Robbed on the Night Shift at Kentucky Fried" and "Lightning Bird"

South Dakota Review: "The Claudia Sanders Dinner House," "Electric Fire," and "White Castle"

Southern Indiana Review: "Breaking Bird" and "Wishbone"

Two Weeks: "Grease Trap"

Vox Populi: A Public Sphere for Politics and Poetry: "Ball and Pivot"

Some of the poems appeared in the chapbook, *Adultery Chicken*, which appeared in *The Blue Mountain Review*. Those poems included "Polyester," "Adultery Chicken," "Learner's Permit," "A Very Special Recipe," "Waiting for the Colonel," "Nine Easy Pieces," "Color-blind," "Good Girls Don't," "Homefront," "Whiffle Hen," "Honey on My Tongue," and "Animated and Extra Crispy™."

I want to dedicate this book to my English 594 class of Spring 2013: Josh Bontrager, Austin Kodra, Zach Macholz, Phil Martin, Andrew McSorley, Lucien Darjeun Meadows, Robert Parrott, and Laura Ruffino. This book wouldn't exist without you.

To my co-workers, thanks for making this possible and me, perhaps, a little wiser.

And to Allison, who kept believing these stories could become poems.

CONTENTS

IV

V

CODA

Life as I Have Known It Has Been Finger Lickin' Good
        —title of the autobiography of Col. Harland Sanders

I

"I think anyone who is a carnivore needs to understand that meat does not originally come in these neat little packages."

—Julia Child

Honest Labor

Meat, one of the assistant coaches called us,
prime meat, as the other guards and tackles ground
into one another with their slow weight and push,
our muscles straining to prove which of us would

freeze as perfect statues locked together
in a grappler's pose, others tumbling back
like unsteady bowling pins marking the unlikely
spare. I was falling off the depth chart that autumn,

former tackle to guard to center to long snapper
on the offensive lineman's path to the bench
and a purple and gold letter jacket earned
for showing up and shutting up. So I punted

football after my fifteenth birthday, and the first
job interview my father drove me to was my last,
filling out the blanks on the form the girl in the white
and red bowl of a hat handed me and I waited

for the curly-haired manager in a crisp white shirt,
black slacks, and black string tie to join me
in the booth, ask me where I went to school,
if I did drugs, if I knew what honest labor was,

knew what hard work demanded and was ready
to do it here for one dollar and sixty-five cents
an hour since a minor like me under sixteen
had a trial period to see if I was mature enough

to take a job seriously. He did like I played football,
said this work involved lifting fifty pound sacks
of flour, seventy-five pound cases of fresh chicken
on ice, but I looked *hearty enough,* he said,

a big enough boy to do the job, if I showed up
at four-thirty the next day wearing jeans and good
work shoes he would have my own red-and-white-
striped shirt ready and I could clock in, watch

training films, maybe do a little dishwashing
since I had told him of the hundreds of campers
whose trays and glasses and silverware I washed
every weekend at the camp my father ran,

the summers I had worked each meal five days
a week. I would start slow here, part-time, he said,
three days a week for five-hour shifts, maybe one
weekend day if I worked out, but I shouldn't

expect much, was young and would need to prove
myself to him, *to earn my wings.* Two weeks later
I got my first raise, in four weeks I was working
twenty hours, then twenty-five, thirty, then

double shifts every weekend and earning overtime,
opening the store those Saturday and Sunday mornings,
shutting it down, blast-washing it clean most nights
until I couldn't imagine another way to end my days.

ELECTRIC FIRE

Breading station to sink
to fryer to cooler to sink
to station to sink to fryer
and back, Andre taught me

and taught me again and again,
his two years cooking almost
over, full-ride scholarship
and college ahead, my time

beginning with no future
beyond the cash to buy a car
when I turned sixteen in what
seemed forever or at least

a teenager's version of
a lifetime away, so I listened
like someone who thought
he knew everything and

on my first close with Dre
I filled the Extra Crispy™
breading station bin with water,
a stainless steel lake of cloudy

depths murky with the day's
dried and caked leavings,
a gummy flotilla on the shivering
surface rippling with every

back and forth of the motor
shaking new white flour
powdered again by the pebbles
of fat grinding and almost sticking

on the sifting screen below.
With paint scraper and steel wool,
I muscled and scoured until
hard dough concrete from

the double breading for crunchy
golden finish turned softer
papier-mâché and finally streaks
of whitewash slime I could wipe

away until the metal mirrors
shined brilliant again, reflecting
the same thing this night reflected
tomorrow or the next, and I was

daydreaming about gods and heroes,
an Edith Hamilton fourth-period
quiz on Hercules, Theseus,
and Perseus, all bastard sons

of Zeus and sure test questions,
when my fingers and hands
pricked with invisible needles
like a thousand strands from

Medusa's hair struck all my skin
at once with serpents' fangs,
poison numbing my touch
each time the yellow rubber

gloves submerged to spin
wider and wider circles with
steel wool in the gray white muck.
From behind, I heard Dre order me

to freeze, stand perfectly still,
and then I saw what he saw,
blue sparks dripping from my
gloves to the bin of water

back up to my fingers,
a hand of light and power
beckoning me, grasping
for our circuit to connect,

take hold, complete the path
leading to ecstatic pain
my nerves couldn't understand
or reject until Dre reached up

above my head to the outlet
descending to meet the black vine
of the breading station's heavy cord,
pulled the fat head of the plug

loose, broke the link chaining
me to the building's cells,
the living grid of alien current
discharged from my soft chaos

of flesh, a creation too fragile
to receive this blessing,
too weak to wear a garment
woven by holy fire, lucky

to survive my carelessness
before putting on a laurel
wreath of industrial lightning
beyond my static human coil.

BREAKING BIRD

You break the thighs, that's all—
a quick snap like you imagine any bone
forced from the joint it's bedded in might give
to pull and twist and pop. The raw meat
under your fingers cool to the touch

like water in the shade of a cliff face
that never feels the sun, like moss
on the underside of a deadfall off a quiet path.
The skin thick like the tongue of a workboot—
nothing like anything once alive should feel

—sliding and sucking in the tightening grip
of your thumb. But that is last. First, there is the tail,
nub of useless stump that feathered the fat
and bony end of these inept flyers,
and you crank it once, twice, mostly never three times

till it gives way in your pinch and you toss it off
into the growing pile in the trash where these clips
of skin and bone collect, each looking like
the first joint of a fleshy thumb that's lost its nail,
naked now, unable to grasp even the smallest thing.

Chicken Dance

Doors with locks,

    doors with nails,

punching clocks,

    punching sacks,

tagging names,

    tagging sides,

blades that grind,

    blades that trim,

weighing flour,

    weighing time,

wringing rags,

    wringing necks,

breaking birds,

    breaking skin,

hands with scars,

    hands with cuts,

scouring blood,

    scouring grease,

sweat from flame,

    sweat from ice,

trays that spill,

    trays that spoil,

cooling oil,

    cooling smiles,

heat with weight,

    heat with steam,

wash that stinks,

    wash that cleans,

wash that cleans,

    wash that stinks,

heat with steam,

    heat with weight.

cooling smiles,

    cooling oil,

trays that spoil,

sweat from ice,

scouring grease,

hands with cuts,

breaking skin,

wringing necks,

weighing time,

blades that trim,

tagging sides,

punching sacks,

doors with nails,

trays that spill,

sweat from flame,

scouring blood,

hands with scars,

breaking birds,

wringing rags,

weighing flour,

blades that grind,

tagging names,

punching clocks,

doors with locks.

LEARNER'S PERMIT

Cruising Rodney Parham to Reservoir
and back in the assistant manager's
late model Cutlass Supreme, fifteen
years old but Randy was twenty-four,
a Mr. Kotter curly hairstyle on top of
a blinding Vinnie Barbarino smile,
and if he'd been watching me instead
of making out with Mary we would
have been technically legal if not
stretching the spirit of the law. But
nothing right was happening here.
I had cleaned the kitchen, Randy made
deposits, and Mary cleaned counters,
warmers, service areas, and we all
finished over an hour before my parents
would come and collect me. Randy
always had two joints rolled and ready
but Mary never joined us and we didn't
need more than one. When Randy
found out I had a learner's permit, he
said he could teach me to drive, but
really he knew if we were rolling no
LRPD would pay any attention to what
was going on in the back seat. I did,
and he began peeling off the white
cotton shirt she had changed out of her
polyester work top like I peeled albums
out of their cellophane at her other
job at the Target on John Barrow Road.
I rode my bike the first couple of times
but figured out if I walked the two miles
from my home she would offer to give
me a ride back in the red VW Beetle
held together with rubber bands. She
liked my company like a little brother

she could teach the way the world
worked and I had never known anyone

whose kindness and beauty blended
like the perfect morning light, a sunrise
warming you just because the day's
promise included everything breathing
and waking to the possibility of being.
As long as I didn't overdo it, she let me
take advantage of her position running
the music department, opening albums
so they became "slightly damaged,"
merchandise now available for a dollar
for regular albums, two dollars for
doubles. It was hard not to strip them
all, and someone should've locked me up
for bad taste—the Bee Gees soundtrack
Sgt. Pepper's Lonely Hearts Club Band,
Barbra Streisand's *Superman* mainly
because I liked the T-shirt, Olivia Newton-
John's *Totally Hot* for the leather, though
luck took me to *Taj Mahal* because I
found the name funny, an Indian palace
built for love and death, was so taken
by the music I added John Lee Hooker
and B.B. King to my shopping list
along with *Briefcase Full of Blues* since
even I knew the Blues Brothers. But
in Randy's car the music playing each
ride his 8-tracks—Boston, The Eagles,
some early "Quiet Storm" tapes to set
the mood for Mary—and I watched more
and more of her skin filling the mirror,
making me feel less and less, even hoping
for the rear view to fill with light from
a car behind us, a flash of brilliance

to turn my soundtrack of failure into
any fantasy I wanted foolishly to believe.

ADULTERY CHICKEN

Faithfulness and flavor need more than salt,
whether from the brow or the table shaker,
so when one of the assistant managers said
rumor was the recipe belonged to a mistress,

not the Colonel, even though the training video
showed the man, familiar white suit and black

string tie, sauntering past the rebuilt Sanders
Court and Café, not original black suit with tails,
gold watch chain, and thousands of miles,
days of handshake deals over plates and plates

of pressure-cooked fried chicken and the best
gravy anyone ever licked off their greasy fingers,

the Colonel's Lady overcoming her shyness
in a yellow antebellum dress serving cole slaw,
mashed potatoes, maybe baked beans, and rolls.
But she was second for his heart, his first wife

from his railroad days and when he stopped
receiving answers to his letters home he returned

to find no furniture, no children or wife there,
her family taking them back in away from him,
thinking she could have done better, and what
became a thirty-nine-year unhappy marriage

proved someone right as sure as when it ended
he married well at last to the woman who made

the beds at his motel and made him believe
there was something he could do with the rest
of his life. So what does it matter if he authored
this combination of measure, taste, and luck

alone or found help and inspiration where
he also found a partner who traveled with him

sometimes, other times met the late-night
train to mail packages of what was probably
plenty of paprika, salt, and the essence of
flavor in Accent, plus a choir of other choices

in harmonies of ground oregano and sage,
garlic powder and onion salt, dried marjoram,

black and white pepper, and the possibilities
of chili powder or cinnamon, basil, cardamom,
nutmeg or any of the other discordant notes
a unique song can bend to its purpose, all

mixed into the clean white field a fifty-pound
bag of flour can spill pure and true time

after time, the chaste surface to welcome
the dirty delicious passion the lips await,
the kiss that once in the mouth new lovers
hunger for again and again without shame.

II

If you're ever in Mexico, be sure to go to the Monterey, Nuevo Leon. There, on the corner of Gonzalitos and Vancouver, you'll find a Kentucky Fried Chicken take home.

—text from the back of the record album
Colonel Sanders' Tijuana Picnic

A VERY SPECIAL RECIPE

The best thing I ever cooked myself
and never will again was beyond off-
the-menu and forbidden, but when
you are fifteen years old and work

sixty-five-hour weeks in summer
frying chicken the number of things
you will listen to that anyone says

you can't do becomes smaller than
the hours you aren't exhausted or
sleeping or back at work again.
We only sold the special Hot &

Spicy™ blend after Memorial Day
until Labor Day, an attempt to keep
Popeyes down in Louisiana where

those Cajun-style flavors closed
down some of the Colonel's long-
time franchises. One of our cooks
experimented with the orange

day-glo chicken pieces that spilled
from the marinator's steel drum
and found that if we used Original

Recipe™ flour rather than the bland
Extra Crispy™ that even the Colonel
called "a damn fried doughball
stuck on some chicken," the result

tasted good in the deep fryers but
became something worth calling
special if we used the Henny Penny

pressure cooker and its little cage
of wire trays to stack a bird or two
into the hot oil bath. We tried every
method we could think of until

finally discovering that double-
breading the Original Recipe™ flour
—a second egg wash dip to pat on

a more luscious coating—gave
us an almost perfect result, but
when one of us thought to cook
only the center breast pieces,

the all-white keel with wishbone
intact, and to stuff the pockets
on each side of the breastbone

with one whole jalapeno pepper,
we had a spicy, moist, savory
dish that was worth filtering
the machine's oil twice to strain out

the flavors we cooked into the meat,
worth every bit of the time and
effort to discover when those hot

juices burst onto your tongue,
coated your lips with a tangy kiss,
almost worth getting fired just
to have the memory of that taste.

POLYESTER

Corporate synthetics unnaturally clinging to our skin,
binding our corporeal selves to the publicly-traded
carefully-branded and re-branded identity of a bucket

of convenience, our sweat each day glued this red-
and-white-striped armor over our true selves hidden
underneath. But most of us shed the uniform first

chance we got after clocking out, peeling away
the sticky fabric like testing a scar to see if living
tissue might be healing underneath, if the heavy

damp net we spent our days drowning in could be
cast off, traded for the clean sharp air and illusions
of freedom. The women and girls working the front

of the store had it worse than the teenage boys behind
them in the kitchen or the childish men disappearing
into the manager's office after each mealtime's rush

with the day's receipts. The managers wore white
shirts with black string ties, black slacks, and black
dress shoes. The cooks wore the candy-striped shirt

and silly crown of a paper peaked cap that never
lasted long, but necessity allowed us jeans and
whatever heavy shoes or boots might save our feet

from the grease and spills and water and heat.
The women, young and older, couldn't escape full
regalia—red polyester slacks tight as a snake's skin,

white shoes, white-and-red-striped apron-like vest
over a red top, and a red-brimmed white newsboy
Gatsby-style hat, a round and fat bubble on top

to conceal fully any shining crown of hair within it.
Whatever our religion these were our vestments
now and until we disrobed, our rituals unfolding

daily in garments proven to resist the visible stains,
the wear and tear sure to mark us in more indelible
ways than any fabric could ever hope to cover up.

WAITING FOR THE COLONEL

The day I met the second best fry cook
in those central Arkansas chicken franchises,
we both were working together in a small
take home store like the hundreds that had
spread the good news of the bucket and
side dishes across the country and the world.

We were used to the kind of restaurants
we usually worked in, sit down spots with
a portrait of the Colonel in a front corner,
pictures of happy families on the walls
smiling and laughing as the perfect Sunday
dinner waited for their prayer, or perhaps

the mother and father and two children—
of course, a boy and girl—had a blanket
down on the grass on a beautiful day
with the full meal and fixings spread out
before them as the Colonel sat nearby
with a bucket of chicken in his lap like

he did on the album cover of *Colonel
Sanders' Tijuana Picnic,* a marketing ploy
to cash in on Herb Alpert's success and
connect the brassy joyous music with
a familiar pastoral scene and the occasion
of stores opening in Mexico in the late '60s.

This location we were in part of a memory
that wouldn't last much longer, low
volume and no seating dooming it to
a sure closing in the near future, but for
this day an all-star crew would create
the illusion of a past perfect in its moment,

where every spot of grease, drop of water,
mote of flour disappeared as soon as we
cooked and prepared each order, a kitchen
where all our efforts seemed effortless
with every surface shining, no dishes
waiting in the sink, our aprons brilliant

white and unsoiled. The Colonel was
downtown at the Chamber of Commerce
luncheon, back in the city he had been
a lawyer with no training practicing before
the Justice of the Peace bench sixty years
ago until brawling in the courtroom

with his own client ended one of so many
careers he pursued, but we were told
he never lost that legendary temper
and knew when he arrived here our purpose
was to present him a store like those he first
opened everywhere for so many years,

our job to keep him from raising his black
cane and beating out his percussive anger
on our spotless counter. So we waited
and worked and cleaned and waited,
erasing our every action in preparation
for a visit that would never happen.

NINE EASY PIECES

Learning a new language of nine,
each plastic-wrapped chilled bird
gave us that ever-odd count again.

Trucks loaded with cold cases on
hot and hotter afternoons where
ice was dead wet weight in our
grips as we challenged one another,
heavy and heavier loads our own

Sisyphean task in another pointless
idiotic work game for boys who
didn't understand the lasting damage
each box added to the body's ledger.

Believing we proved something
real when two, three, or maybe
even four seventy-five-pound boxes
anchored our sinking arms as we
stumble-walked forward with
three hundred reasons to break down.

Wax-coated boxes slick in our hands,
impervious to water and our sweat,
numbed our fingers into frozen
grasping claws that bent to lift again.

Cases piled five high in the walk-in,
each rack two deep, the boxes of
new chicken in back all filled with
twenty fresh birds, hoping we had
enough weekend business before
rot and stink replaced clean dead air.

Blood and water drained from
racks to the floor, and we watched
every degree the thermometer
added each time the door opened,
salmonella waiting at forty
to bloom and spoil all our work.

We knew heat killed the waste
incubating inside so we hurried all
nine pieces from egg wash to flour to
glorious cleansing four hundred degrees.

Splatter and pop of deep fryers,
ingenious pressure cookers sealing in
dark secrets of heat and oil, answer
everyone mistook for herbs and spice.

Bucket after bucket filled with our
roll call of one center breast, two
each of side breasts—really just
awkwardly-cut back the Colonel
split to make three white pieces from
two—to join thighs, legs, and wings.

Tricks of the trade, each bird now
having nine parts to sell, not eight,
innovation by slick country cooks
getting every penny, every little bit
helping to stretch the valuable meat.

Leftovers almost always wings and
extra thighs, the hard sells we'd
gather at night, a last inventory of waste.

FAMOUS HOT GRAVY™

The code of flavor burns
in the bottom of a grease bath,
flour and fat, pepper and salt,

the spices and the grease again
though the filters run every
third batch, run again and again

as the hot trays fill and empty
with bird upon bird. But soon
the silt of flavor builds

in the white bucket you tuck
back in the walk-in until
the roiling water's ready

and you stir essence back
and add the corporate secret—
the binder of food starch,

maltodextrin, and the rest
hydrolyzed, modified, and
artificial, with not more than

two percent silicon dioxide
added as an anti-caking agent.
And the flavor of packaging

the heat transfers, the flavor
of heat itself sets and skins
over until the surface breaks

and the memory of roux
and right and wrong burns
the top of your mouth, tempts

the tip of your tongue
and you pour it on
despite your best intentions.

III

This *is* the day *which* the LORD hath made; we will rejoice and be glad in it.

—Psalm 118:24

THIS DAY THE LORD

We gathered around locked glass doors, waiting to
start our Sunday service preparing to serve, not

with reverent hymns and desperate prayers, knowing
good news for us a one-day special coupon sale cut

fresh from the morning's heavy newspapers, promising
chicken in nine or fifteen or twenty-one pieces,

like five loaves and two fish, an endless banquet
we could feed the four thousand, five, or even more,

know the buckets would reappear again full as long as
we kept performing our rituals like we knew we

should. We were all apostates before these flames.
Eleven o'clock and we welcomed in the first wave,

herbs the incense of this perfumed air heavy with gravy
and boiling ears of corn, baked beans on the stove top,

spices peppering every sweet corner hunger can
make desire, can make fat and happy believe anything

it needs can be wrapped in wax paper, wipe grease from
finger to lips to tongue, a nation of thirsty worshipers

licking the salt until all could behold it, and it was
good. Abundance as long as the electricity stayed on.

We knew the cost of waste, the ledgers our bosses would
use as punishment if we dropped or spilled, turned

fresh into spoiled, and we feared the wrath from burning
chicken, missing the clarion of the buzzer set for thirteen,

not fourteen, minutes, potatoes drying out, cole slaw
frozen or sour, the plastic bags of rolls soggy or crispy.

It's a miracle there was any food at all those days when
the world around us was designed for every disaster, the

Colonel's face everywhere we turned, mocking us with its
secret knowledge that our faith was misplaced, our

recipe was a recipe for unpaid bills, a path to a future
that would cover us with scars and pain, the failure that

makes an apostle a heretic, takes hard work and turns
it into less than pocket change, fills the mouth with the

taste of blood and sweat, a metallic tang behind your teeth
so sharp and false, so unnatural that nothing can taste

good. Could we cash our checks and tithe ourselves?
Not for nothing, but something less and less we

chopped and peeled until the skin was either ours
or the birds', the trays and trays of a country of fowl

rolled from grease to warmer, a procession for quick feast
or ending the famine of home cooking, the clock's hands

frozen; faster than family, generations and the new hearth,
it's all television-ready and friendly, the golden crisp

chicken, the smiling counter girls and young men with
nothing on their minds but the bright gleaming gospel of

more. Feed you, fill you, find the limit of all appetites.
And if that isn't enough, we have dessert! Chocolate

that's not chocolate, but chocolate creme, lemon creme,
the strawberry shortcake with more creme, but no

real strawberries that seem like fruit, all sweet and
good if you don't know better. There is never any

reason to leave with empty hands or stomachs wanting
more because we have it all here to satisfy and stuff

folks from city to suburbs to farm, young and old
come to our counter and receive our blessings, drive

through our convenient pick-up window and know
our generosity, the grace that will follow you to your

door. Speak clear, speak loud so we can hear you say,
"I'm ready to order. Is anyone there?" Know we are

coming, we are here, we cannot leave and are trapped
in this kitchen until the last one has ordered, when no

more customers wait for the next fryer to empty
and the next, for the coupons to expire and be no

more than tomorrow's trash, no more value than confetti
for a forgotten parade, the betting slips for the sixth-place

Kentucky Derby finish. Give us this, freely, leave us the
fried dreams that stalk our nights, the graveyard full of

chicken. No ghost haunts quite like a skinless silent bird.
It's not forgiveness that is our bargain or our dream,

so many nights where scalding the flesh would feel
nice, if only the water could be hot enough, the heat

nice if it could boil out of each pore that smell, that chain
to the kitchen linking our bones to the birds' so we

feel, not dirty, not grimy, but seared from the inside
so the vision of our sacrifice isn't crucifixion, no

good for the world in our losses, but we feel cooked,
about to be served to something angry in its hunger,

a shadow of vengeance that will have us as its rightful
meal, and there isn't enough, never enough for that,

so we must forget it, deny there are such dreams, say
good night once the floors are cleaned, only talk

about tomorrow's day off or the day after, wonder if
Kentucky is that different from Arkansas, if everything's

fried there like most things are here, if their catfish and
hushpuppies and green tomatoes are better than their chicken.

INSECTICIDE: THE FOUR-WAY TEST

"…a few years later the Four-Way Test of Rotary came along. A man ought not be permitted to go in business unless he can abide by that test. Least I don't think he'll amount to very much if he doesn't."

—Col. Harland Sanders, *Life As I Have Known It Has Been Finger Lickin' Good*

Flour and water, blood, meat and grease, trash and more trash, there is
no end to what feeds upon what the business of hunger brings with it
through every crack and crevice, each door open or simply ajar, the
highway of drains where the silverfish and cockroaches know the truth

of our failures, the swarms of flies breeding where the building is
spitting out its garbage day and night. Exterminate, fumigate, spray it
over and over again, this feedyard teeming with multitudes, a state fair
where the attractions leave a choking cloud behind, a wild ride trying to
balance the cost of safety and poison. Our most loyal consumers all
have six legs, here when we open each morning, they aren't concerned

we close since their best hours come while we're away, they will
find everything we hide, fill our traps, bring us grime and grief until it
is water rising against our efforts, destroying any dam we try to build
to contain the flood. No armistice in this war we are losing, no goodwill
given by either side, the dead too many to count on one, the sick and
tired on the other weary and disgusted. Perhaps surrender would be better
than the creeping gas filling our trenches, our only battlefield friendships

between the masks and our noses and mouths, the goggles we hope will
keep our eyes from burning in the haze. Fire could cleanse this, but it
is not an option, too much insect city to burn and then what would be
left behind but ash and metal, charred carapaces, nothing beneficial
in such madness, so every morning we patrol again, our mission to
search and destroy the colonies thriving in our sovereign state, all
our efforts a temporary stay we execute to reassure anyone concerned.

GOD OF THE KITCHEN

Somewhere, emerging from four-hundred-degree fryers,
skittering and popping with ethereal heat and pain,
it rises like an Aztec god of fear and holy retribution,

but where feathers should cloak its back and shoulders
with royal luminescent plumage, cascade its wings
in a plush coat of white so pure and blinding like

the perfect ermine fur dreams to be, instead a golden
crispy skin still crackles from the bath of roiling,
singing grease. The beak's cruel scimitar glints toward

us like the useless tongs we raise now, dull tools
to pull the first pieces floating to the top as heavy
thighs still nestle in the oil before a last ascent to light

and steam. Our ghost, our king pinches us in its fierce
grip, shakes us dry and clean of sweat and flour and hope
before we are cut open, emptied of heart and liver

and all the rest spilling to the floor's drains, butter-
flied and separated into our nine or eight pieces,
neck and head magically disappearing as the offering

of herbs and spices, fat and bone and blood and flesh
are spread forth, arranged by parts and pieces on silver
trays waiting for worship in these altars of warming air.

WISHBONE

A handshake with pain,
under the palm's fleshy
bunker sandbagging
muscle and nerve below
the soft knot swollen
with heat in a hot summer

of breading and frying,
frying and breading,
and so much soapy water
in sinks and buckets
that the spongy wrinkled
skin like the dead birds'

skin feels right feeling
wrong, and so it's only
when your hand begins
to look like a blued filet,
scars marking sears from
grease and flame, and

your fingers have fattened
like plumping franks
on the end of a campfire
skewer, you begin rubbing
the delta of the thumb
and index finger, the nexus

of the pain you have ignored
for a week, week and a half
at most, and you feel a thin
bone where there is no bone—
no bone of yours at least—
a needle stitching its way

inside the tight knitting
of your muscle and blood,
and you keep massaging
its line of nerve fire until
you find the tender point
of this inch-long splinter

and against the tongue-
biting, eye-searing scream
of each measure of renewed
press and push a point
finally breaks back out
of what you imagined was

your closed skin, an old
wound open you thought
nothing more than a scratch
when a chicken bone from
the keel, the center breast
cut from beneath the bird's

tender rib cage, knifed
so quietly inside, curving
within the pocket hiding
under your thumb until
infection protested this
invasion, burning out

what never belonged in
and you slowly pull on
the end hoping it will all
hold together and through
the pus and blood it does,
and when you wash it clean,

your hand cleansed over
and over in steamy lather
and soaking in a bowl full
of alcohol until all the heat
is gone, you realize you
hold in your other hand

the short end of a wishbone,
a failure like so many
you don't yet see ahead,
now only a curiosity and
caution that won't slow
you down soon enough.

In the Hall of the Mountain King

The grease wore me like a golem-child,
cousin raised from clay, blood, and sweat
melting all night to a puddle for morning.

Sixteen-hour summer shifts pressure frying
cemeteries' worth of bird for the Colonel
closed each day near midnight with steam-

hoses then a joint or two blazing beneath
the empty parking lot's bug-crowned lights.
At home in the basement cave I'd helped

build separate from bumper pool and foosball,
I locked my flimsy door, stripped off the red-
and-white-striped shirt, pried free steel-toe

boots, peeled away sodden jeans and socks
and shorts from my fish-white puckered flesh.
I tasted bleach in my dreams. But I was wired

every night, nailed between deep fatigue
and adrenaline like the pine two-by-fours
and wallboard that slapped up this refuge.

Sometimes turkey dope and whiskey
cut behind the edge of tension our family doctor
prescribed useless Soma for, then Quaaludes

that friends on the bus crushed up to snort
on the long ride over to Horace Mann Jr. High
all spring. But these summertime seventy-hour

weeks cashed in overtime and nothing else.
Then one morning I remembered the Great Bøyg
and *Song of Norway*, a forgettable film I'd seen

with my grandmother almost eight years before,
and I went out, bought Grieg's incidental music
for *Peer Gynt*. She had died that April and I

felt like death, felt like a buried child lost
under a mountain, and this troll-song, this
unlikely lullaby, bassoons and cellos, stillness

and stuttering forward, the frenzied rising
to timpani rumble and cymbal explosions
excavated my mind from its stone tomb.

Color-blind

I thought the chickens lived in black and white,
but who was I to think I knew anything about
anything, avoiding the only question anyone

sensible would have asked those years I went
from high school to kitchen to bed to summer
to kitchen to bed and eventually back to class

only to know I was hiding why in every minute
clocked and paid regular and time and a half.
Why did I work forty hours and more as other

high school students put in fifteen or twenty
for spending money on dates, a little extra
to put away for college? I bought a strange

little automatic Honda Civic with a hole
in the floorboard but a removable backseat
that could hide bottles, bags, a life I led

beyond straight A's except for the nine weeks
I slept through trigonometry and took a D
only to ace the other three quarters after a day

the teacher suggested everyone leave me,
head down on my desk snoring when class
ended, but I heard him and popped up to his

and the students' surprise, said, "I don't think
so." He swore I had been sound asleep, but truly
I never was, always on the edge of a waking dream

as undiagnosed sleep apnea grew worse and more
soul-consuming for another decade. My father
had lost his seventeen-year job here and Mother

needed a paycheck for the first time in my life,
brother and sister away at Hendrix College
on half-tuition Methodist ministers' children

received from my father's thirty years now
lost, but I had never been a problem—band,
football, glee club, even Eagle Scout behind—

and now a model worker still succeeding
and in the Honor Society. But I turned down
Arkansas Boys State because they wouldn't allow

cars and I wanted to commute from Conway
so I wouldn't miss a week of work. My first
summer I worked sixty, seventy, even one week

of eighty-four hours, but the next summer,
when I was seventeen, I almost reached
perfection in my deep-fried mind when I

worked six days seven A.M. until midnight,
forty regular and sixty-two hours of overtime,
one hundred and two hours even drawing notice

from our district manager, who said never let
that happen again. You could have branded
the red and white stripes on my skin those days

I was so lost in the prison I built for myself
from grease and bones and blood. But my why
was the cause of an effect of something else,

something I did not see. The chickens see more
colors than we do, an extra cone in their eyes
making ultraviolet paint bugs and feed and other

birds, showing hens an egg we will never see,
the rooster a sunrise with beauty we can only
imagine in a virtual existence. But we have

tried to blind the birds for commerce, placing
glasses with red lenses on to make them
docile, eat less, more productive, upsetting

the natural pecking order, even moving on
to contact lenses since the glasses fell off,
but blinding the birds wasn't the answer,

infections and death bad for the bottom line.
When I trained to be a fry cook, Tony and Dre
were older African American young men

crossing Little Rock—one from Granite
Mountain, where opportunities were hard
as the stone coming out of the quarries,

the other from Little Rock's purposefully-
named Confederate Boulevard—making
our store on Rodney Parham integrated

more naturally than our schools, white
and black churches. I saw the uniform
and little else, but the more I worked,

the hours that more and more appeared
with my name assigned on the schedule
beside the time clock, the other cooks

became whiter and then front counter
workers and servers until the entire crew
was all the same, and I realize now the first

White domino to fall was me, managers one
by one consciously or not turning us into
a sixties version of the company's television

fantasies of Lady Godiva in her pinkish leotard
riding through the countryside with a bucket
of chicken and a smile, only a yellow tabby

to look askance at her spectacle, but I was our
convenient aberration and distraction, nakedly
consuming so many opportunities for others

with my unnatural obsession, as blind to what
was happening as a pacified bird, and so tired,
so very tired, I wore my lenses for years.

IV

full-thickness burn – a burn involving destruction of the entire skin; deep full-thickness burns extend into subcutaneous tissue, muscle, or bone and often cause much scarring.

— *Farlex Partner Medical Dictionary*

WINGS OF SKIN

Somewhere between Geyer Springs Road
and Robinson Auditorium I left the earth
for a place where red lights turned green
and *Die Fledermaus* and The Knack's

"My Sharona" fused into a teenaged rat
whose skin peeled off his fingers from
the night before's burning. But this end
of the story came late after Sunday's

twelve-hour shift and the deep well of dead
air in my mind when the assistant manager,
Debra, left the receipts to find me standing
at the fryer like it was the three-compartment

sink and I casually rinsed my hands in
the filtering grease like a spigot I thought
poured out coolness before me. Fortunately,
the flames were out and the heat now half

its four hundred degrees, but my swelling
hands still stung and blistered while the cold
water and soap she rinsed them with cut
the grease and left me with two pink clubs.

I had the next night off, a school night
with tickets to the Arkansas Symphony
Orchestra and extra credit, but Debra
said her husband had something special

and I figured both were possible if I left
early enough. Sometimes special is
an understatement, and after three bowls
driven deep with a shot of nitrous oxide

to propel me beyond the edge of their
fake ferns and real plants, the music
in the background like Technicolor
wallpaper, her hair brushing over my

shoulder on the leather couch, his hands
clapping to the beat of his laughter when
he realized they still had some acid left
somewhere in the bedroom, I remembered

my second engagement and saw where
this was going, saw a place I'd never leave
if I wandered onto that hypnotic stage,
a night I wouldn't find my way home.

LIVERS AND GIZZARDS

Water the secret to these offal
simple recipes, the wet dark blood
soaking the spongy organ no weight
of pungent flavor could hold against
the splatter of angry grease flying
from the roiling clouds of the fryer
like arcing bolts of sear and burn
fusing heat's tattoo script on skin.
But the muscle of grist softens
in the pressure of steam's boil
until the whistle valve spits forth
the stinging mist of essence's stink,
the knot of chew readying its rubber
gravel pop for the willing mouth
through a slow crusted sink and
rise in the surface of the gold bath.
Both wait and wait for that special
tongue, mother wit hungry for half-
or full pints of one, the other, or
sometimes both, transitory crispy
nuggets sweating and drying out
until gut goes to gut or trash, when
what is thrown away is prized or lost.

How Not to Get Robbed on the Night Shift at Kentucky Fried

Someone has more than chicken on the mind these summer nights.
Lock the doors. Not at ten-o-one or -two. Close the lobby
but don't pull down the shades till three—you want the cars to see
you mopping in your red-and-white-striped shirt. But don't forget
someone has more than chicken on the mind these summer nights.
Check the peephole three times at least before you turn the bolt
and drag the heavy trash across the lot to the dumpster
close to the walk-in Taco Bell that gets held up each week.
Knock four times then two then four again to get back inside.
Someone has more than chicken on the mind these summer nights.

WHITE CASTLE

Not the porcelain enamel bright
as everything meat isn't, boys

shining crisply in white uniforms
with every button gleaming

beyond polished stainless steel
exteriors, interiors cutting and

dealing light like hand after hand
of miracle cards flashing money-

dreams over a spilling stack of chips;
no, our "white castle" had no turrets,

no splendor, no gallant illusion
when box after box of wax paper-

wrapped opaque bricks of tenderly
heavy hydrogenated vegetable oil

filled the deep wells of each fryers'
warming pit where soft white bars

disappeared into gold on gold on
silver heat shimmering with lies

of purity and the dark hot truth
lurking with a monster's branding

tongue, teeth of splatter, and breath
of smoke and steam until the brown

coffee liquid aged and fired its way
back to this melt again every thirty

or forty days. Those long nights
when we turned over the grease

like a black lake spilling winter's
secrets to the sunlight of spring

to find the fish frost-burned and
the water still ice-cold and sterile,

the renderers' fifty-five gallon
drums swelled with the potential

of every bucket we poured out
and as we unwrapped each slick

package I imagined those bricks
building the store, one greasy layer

after another piling into white walls
beneath the pale glow of moon

and stars until the warm pilot light
of dawn fires and a drizzle of oil

becomes a slippery rain, a shower
of gold into a downpour drowning

the parking lot, the street, the land
as far as it reached into the swamp

of sludge we swam in every day,
that swims, settles inside our hearts.

GOOD GIRLS DON'T

Friday and Saturday July nights,
we wanted things to get sticky
sweet, even just late-night drive-thru

blurry skin shows after we refilled
sodas soon transmuted to rum

or Jack or vodka and Coke, Sprite
and Seven, Southern Comfort and
just about anything, our adolescent

dreams, schoolboy lust filling ten
to one A.M. when only male cooks

and assistant managers worked
since we were waiting for a holdup
that never came. Instead our stupid

macho bravado screamed through
the slow hours between customers

coming or going from odd-hour
shifts themselves or the munchies
and the young women we worked

beside the rest of the long days
entertaining us or their own needs.

Even with the promise of the gun,
we fought over that drive-thru,
knowing Shelly would pull up

in her mom's baby-blue T-Bird
with the latest star football player

or student body second-tier official
who heard she was fast, yes, pretty
fast, but he didn't know she took

what she wanted, discarded men
like men dumped girls, wearing

skintight jeans she had slithered
into with me in the Women's room
girded against my embarrassment

with pre-spandex spandex, my
eighth-grade football pants minus

the pads that I wore under my jeans
to protect me from chafing after
back-to-back day and night shifts

in the swamp of the kitchen
that also served to hide hard-ons

when Shelly stood before me with
only bra and panties since I was
safe. We could also count on

Madeline to appear two or three
times in a bikini top and cut offs

that wouldn't have made it past
network standards and practices
on *The Dukes of Hazzard*, Madeline,

a girl I'd known since she was six
or seven at Markham Methodist

when she barely cast a shadow,
now with a body that made sin
out of a Sunday dress, who thought

kindness was letting us see all
her tan lines and then some.

Or Barbara and her station wagon
full of half-drunk or high, laughing
Mount St. Mary's girls mooning

or flashing us if they didn't know
the guy who won the window.

On summer weekday mornings
when Margaret and Sue gossiped
between mothering and shaming

us and making vats of coleslaw,
potato salad, enough baked beans

for Ann-Margret to take her *Tommy-*
inspired bath. I wasn't spared when
they tore into the rest of us, but

they expected so little of the men
and we didn't often disappoint.

But the girls got it much worse:
*should have known better, needs
to get on the pill, had it coming.*

Shelly got the brunt of their disdain
and I tried to redirect the conversation

since she was my sort of best friend,
had pulled me out of class that spring,
drove me to the Target parking lot

and sat there silently until she finally
spoke in a whisper, "I'm pregnant."

We never slept together, even months
later when she was my prom date
or the last night we saw each other

when after she left I fell into a solipsistic
nightmare and took all the aspirin

in the apartment, thirty-seven measly
tickets only enough to travel a third
of the way, and in a moment of lucidity

called my brother, who introduced me
to ipecac syrup and a night of retching,

but this is about Shelly and her need
for someone to hold her while she
talked about the expensive procedure

in Dallas she'd need to make everything
all right at that late a date. No, I didn't

tolerate much badmouthing of Shelly
and since in their kinder moments
Margaret and Sue thought my sixteen-

year-old self was "husband material"
they let go what I expect might have

been their favorite material. But
they shouldn't have spared us men—
the young assistant manager who

told one of the fifteen-year-olds
he really liked the way a microphone

looked in her hand; Jack, the oldest
cook, trapping anyone female not
Sue or Margaret against counters,

walls, doors and while copping a feel
telling them he was "an ass man";

one of the nicest assistants, Doug,
a forty-five-year-old who couldn't
get ahead in food service but would

always buy beer or hard liquor when
we wanted so we knew he was cool,

gathering guys around to show off
nude Polaroids of his girlfriend,
sixteen years old, the pictures he said

her mother, a close friend, took for him;
but the worst was probably Carl,

who so matter-of-factly stood
behind the closed and bolted back door
when the young women went out

with the trash from the dining area
and demanded a squeeze or pinch

to let them back in the store to finish
their shifts like he was entitled, and to
get on with their night most gave in.

Criminals, perverts, idiots, all of us
guilty by commission or of omissions

daily where we might have demanded
another stop it, but we didn't until
it became clear no one wanted to hear

us sing that song unless the verses
included a sniggling smirk and a wink,

ignoring damage that never goes away
though I hope some of us couldn't erase
the sad stain, carry it still. I do.

FULL THICKNESS

New oil has a deceptive beauty,
a pool shimmering gold, deep
as the mystery of heat, hiding
the kiss of flame, no smoke point
short of five hundred degrees
to warn the unsuspecting cook

of danger, pain, the potential
to burn so great, so certain, yet
unseen until an accidental touch

becomes another level, a new
understanding. I wasn't tired,
no excuse of fatigue, my shift
barely beginning when I started
another quiet Saturday with
the mid-afternoon headed toward

busier evening and close, and
I was touching up the lunch crew's
leavings, a little flour here, trays

in the sink to wash, and the fryer
needing a scraping to clear off
the crust left above the line
where the chicken turned crisp
in the dark bath, but this fryer
had clean new oil and I wondered

why the cook before me put
the white blocks of vegetable oil
into a fryer with this dirty ring

around its collar. Still, it looked
cool when I slid the scraper down
the stainless steel wall and what
I thought was hard and cooked on
wasn't, my hand's force finding
no resistance and I was suddenly

immersed in the purest heat I hope
I'll ever know, my hand and half
my forearm plunging into a full

four hundred degrees. Later,
they would show me the place
on the wall where the scraper
I threw across the room stuck,
better than any shuriken or
sharp throwing knife I played with

as a boy ever did, but in those first
moments after I knew nothing
but the sure sense the fire consumed

every feeling I had until only searing
self-immolating pain, a pain I still
see in my mind as the most primal
howling whimpering thing wanting
nothingness, death, relief from every
hurt balled up in this one hurt, this

shrieking erasure of all self, all sense
of being. The next thing I knew
from that moment was I sat back

in the walk-in cooler, my burned
hand in a plastic bag filled with ice,
and I was breaking chicken, waiting
until a replacement cook came in
to take my place, still on the clock.
I suppose I was in shock, must have

agreed to this though I really don't
recall anything between the burn and
the time I looked down at the raw

chicken in my hands, my hand
in the sack of ice and thought
the meat looked better, closer
to being alive, the crease between
my thumb and index finger over-
cooked like a chicken wing too

long in the fryer, then the colors
that no skin should ever have
leading up to the enormous boil

on my arm, something wrong
that left me thinking this couldn't
be mine, be part of me, and I stared
and broke the chicken thighs until
that boil broke, and all the fluids
and blood and skin filled that bag

of ice and I got up and left my job
to find someone, anyone in the store
who could clean my wounds, put

something over this now scoured
new thing that was my arm before
the air brought back the pain, wrap
me up like something neither living
nor dead until my father or mother
could come and take me home again.

V

Here and there the grease and filth have caked solid, and the creek looks like a bed of lava; chickens walk about on it, feeding, and many times an unwary stranger has started to stroll across, and vanished temporarily.

—Upton Sinclair, *The Jungle*

HOMEFRONT

A scene no Norman Rockwell would ever paint,
my mother sat in the recliner across from me
while, sometime after midnight, I shook my heavy
steel toe boots one after the other off sodden feet
drenched in another day and night's long shift,

but I had forgotten what I had hidden away in that
second one, so while the boot went right toward
my mother, a bag of the finest leaf marijuana
went to the left and my eyes didn't move a bit
in that telling direction as I continued to talk

to her about how things had gone at work,
when I would need to get up that Sunday morning
to return to another long day those summers
I brought home nearly two hundred a week
after taxes, forty hours plus overtime a constant,

and so was the weed, my need growing and
my tastes expensive for 1980, a week's pay not
unusual for me to spend on any number of strains
of homegrown or foreign sensimilla that I'd
break down and mix with Colombian Gold or

Chocolate Thai, Black Magic African, Buddha
stick (though that was sometimes too good to mix),
and always the Panama Red around, cleaning
the herb of all the seeds and stems until only leaf
remained and I would blend different versions

for smooth or strong, a mellow high or oblivion,
whatever the night called for, but I never smoked
at home or alone since it was not difficult to find
someone at work to share such fine weed after
the labor of the day and night had left us spent.

By this point, my father had lost his job as camp
director—the camp the only home I had known
since birth—and we had moved from the United
Methodist church's house in those pine woods
to this rented duplex across from St. Vincent's

Hospital, my birthplace in Little Rock. My mother
had three teenagers to look after as my father tried
to rebuild a professional life for himself after
so many years working for the Board of Global
Ministries Women's Division, and he stumbled

at first in the world of for-profit nursing homes,
his spirit not built for capitalism's end of the line
at the end of life. I was never a problem they
could see, straight-A student going from work
to school and back, most of my scars healing

quickly as my arms and hands shed most hurts
like a snake's skin, new pink flesh appearing
in days or weeks from even the worst the kitchen
could give me. I took pre-college courses in
electronics, out-scored most in my high school

on national math tests when I was a sophomore,
and no one noticed I was a bad idea because
on paper I looked so good. But a high tolerance
for pain and the ability to smile the emptiness
inside away when fatigue and sleeplessness

were all I really felt from each time I punched out
until I punched in again was eating me away
from the inside like the leftovers I brought home
every few nights would be gone the next day
or the next. We talked until there was nothing

more to say that night, and, when we finished,
I said goodnight, got up from the yellow sofa
that had been part of a spotless sitting room
in the camp's house (since at least the furniture
was ours), and as I crossed the room to retrieve

my boots, I scooped up the bag in the same
motion, and there was nothing left to do
but make my way back down into the dark
to find my bed and sleep until what was left
of morning passed and I was back at work again.

BALL AND PIVOT

Jerry looked better than any hog-faced man should,
a Porky Pig grin always on his face, happy to meet
us each time he came around to fix what had broken.

He knew torque and the mechanisms of heat
that kept our kitchens working, the assistant to
the ex-Merchant Marine who was the high priest

to the mysteries Jerry studied, these two heavy men
ministered across the central Arkansas chicken
franchise empire, putting us all back to work when

again and again a pressure valve blew and rained
scorching grease across the exhaust vents and ceiling,
when choking smoke or bubbling sewage stench

filled the kitchen's air and drove us out, when what
was cold was too hot or what demanded heat was
too cold, their gruff grunting bitching voices called

forth whatever metal secrets they both knew and we
were fully ignorant of and they healed the sad sick
store so we could return to our yoke of business.

But Jerry needed more than his assistant's salary
provided, a wedding and honeymoon approaching,
so he joined me on Friday and Saturday nights,

some extra hours for him helping me cook and clean.
I met his fiancé, a perfect Petunia to his Porky,
and his smile grew even brighter reflecting hers,

so I minded much less after meeting her that he
was paid three times what I made for following
my lead, his maintenance rate eleven dollars

an hour while I saw only three fifty at my best pay.
He hated washing dishes, the trays and wire racks
plastered with dried flour or slick with an evening's

layer of grease, so I took the sink while he sprayed
the red brick tile with the steam hose, pushing
before him all the grime and soapy bleach water

toward the drain mouths at the back of the store.
He yelled out to me, something I don't remember,
and I turned to see him spill forward, his left knee

leading the full weight of his body to the floor
and the point exploded with a shotgun blast, his
knee shattered and his screams following as he

rolled over in a heap of tears and pain. I called out
for help and the two girls working that night and
the assistant manager came running as I took

every clean towel I could find, piled most of them
under his head as a pillow and then began gently
wrapping the others around his blood-soaked jeans

where I could feel some sharp points of bone trying
to poke through the fabric. No matter how we pleaded,
we couldn't convince the panicked assistant manager

to call for an ambulance, so he pulled his truck to
the back of the store and the two of us lifted Jerry up,
carried him to the bed of the truck where the girls

had spread clean aprons and towels to make a soft
pallet for Jerry to lie on. One of the girls got in back
with Jerry and the assistant manager drove them all

to the nearest hospital, leaving the other girl and me
with the keys to the store so we could finish closing,
so I could wash Jerry's blood down the waiting drain.

GREASE TRAP

The places the things in this world go to die
hide off to the side, around the corner, under
your feet; and in August, in Little Rock,
someone has to pull up the concrete catch
and bend over like a penitent kneeling down
into the ugly, into the slough too dirty,
too solid, too rotten even for the sewers,
siphoning off the thick fetid swill of cooking
oil, of chicken bone and tattered flesh
the steam hose flushed down the drains
night after day after week after month;
and there is no other way, no machine
as cheap and available as a metal pitcher
and a hand dipping back from the deep
hole to filling bucket; and the rubber gloves
won't keep the smell of how it all goes bad
from the pockets in your lungs, from your
mouth and skin and ears—yes, you can hear
the worst smell you hope you'll never lean
into again—, and the rendering that began
when each spill and scrap touched floor inside
the restaurant ferments inside the fifty-five-
gallon drums inside the truck hauling
the gelling mass away to be turned into
soap and flavoring oils, and this stays inside
you, in the core of where you see and touch
and taste and smell what we leave behind.

Risen

Because on Friday we filled the metal tomb
of the walk-in refrigerator with the bodies
and blood of hundreds of birds flightless
and naked in their waxed heavy cardboard
sarcophagi, resting on a sea of melting ice.

Because on Saturday every corner of each
wire shelf crowded with slaw, potato salad,
three- and baked beans, and the sweet parfaits
gleaming in their plastic cups, and the walls
of spongy rolls and mountain of flour sacks

and herbs-and-spices mix and the rest
of the dry goods waited for the cock's crow.
Because come Sunday morning our sunrise
service on the year's second-busiest day—
not quite honoring mothers but better than

giving thanks on the third day—, our gleaming
start in the shining stainless and spotless
squeaky floor and untouched waiting counters
shattered with a first popping and steaming
metal chariot transporting the twenty golden

birds fried together at once in the great machine
of pressure, grease, and elements of remarkable
heat swayed, wavered, and suddenly crashed
down when a shaky wheel found an open drain
left uncovered the night before during the last

cleansing wash as someone hosed away a long
day's leavings, and now, like a horse might
stumble when a hoof sinks in a rabbit hole,
this weight headed earthward, uncertain
ground and gravity too much to overcome

and what should have been safe in ready
warmers scattered in a scorching slick mess.
Because the front doors would not be open
for another hour, we knelt down, gathered
back together each tray and every part

of the collateral chickens from the scene
of the accident, nested the trays back
in their crib of metal, and we returned them
to their searing bath for two quick minutes,
knowing the machine's heat could purify,

knowing resurrection may be real but came
with the price of faith and filtering the hot oil,
knowing these breasts and legs and wings
and thighs would disappear before anyone
would have a chance to testify to the truth.

WHIFFLE HEN

Beside the dumpster rotten with last night's wet trash,
every morning that infernal August week I pulled in
right next to the red Corvette of the sweetest assistant-

now-turned-manager of her own store on Asher Avenue
in my teenager's attempt to let this woman know
I cared—but more than cared, I understood the petty

evil way the district manager promoted her to shut her up,
to show the high-school-dropout boy-men running
his other stores that a woman with a college degree,

especially a black woman, couldn't run this location.
And he was right, but not like he'd say. The store was
fast food's version of the *Kobayashi Maru* test, no

realistic chance for anything but absolute, utter failure
inside this sweatbox where the kitchen temperature
climbed each day past one hundred and thirty degrees

around four o'clock and then got hotter, a furnace where
no one but stupid me would stay to keep the fryers on.
Even draped in frozen towels about my head and neck,

screen-door fan blasting in the useless Arkansas breeze,
cooking felt like what I was doing inside-out, my hands,
arms, chest, stomach, and legs now Extra Crispy™ or

perhaps Original Recipe™, but I believed I could not fail,
a charm like Bernice, the Whiffle Hen of Thimble Theatre
that Castor Oyl and Popeye rubbed clean of feathers

for her luck on their voyage with Ham Gravy to Dice
Island's casino, Castor winning so much that a gangster
peppered Popeye with bullets and only Bernice's magic

miraculous fortune saved him. But I was no more good
here than a naked bird, just another spoiling thing going
in and out of the walk-in, and on the last day of her trial

period everyone else called in sick and the Pulaski County
Health Department shut us down until a "safer work
environment was provided." She understood how the game

had been rigged against her and resigned, never again
worked for them, but I hadn't learned my lesson yet,
went back to the old store. I thought a winner never quit.

LIGHTNING BIRD

Every night at closing, the brick red tile
floor flooded, a swamp of soap and steam

and bleach, so each kitchen outlet reached
down from our fluorescent heaven of
the stark godless ceiling with 120 volts

of possibility and problem. So many heavy
cords snaking up like black vines climbing

the greasy air to their rapt connections,
male/female bond reproducing alternating
push and pull of stainless steel electric

tables shimmying their sifting snow banks
of clumping flour before the glue of egg,

milk powder, and water left only papier-
mâché strips of random skin and bloating
fat behind. Spinning its ocean web of salt-

water into the ever-thirsty flesh of the bird,
the marinator tried to tumble away on its

own wild ride, the boxy motor on shaky
wheels carrying the out-of-tune steel drum
full of bumping birds from walk-in to kitchen

and back, so we knotted tight one dry towel
after another, securing the unruly plug

to its home in the outlet above until some-
body forgot and I reached up to grab
a damp clean conductor demanding my

sudden cymbal crash of shock and stun
to floor—an avalanche of weighted power

crushing my inner light beneath the world's
singe and spark and flash of deafening heat.
When my ears could see again, my eyes

heard the polyester angels descending
with bright faces of forever now trying

to reshape a clay familiar with something
finding shudder, hesitate, pause, playback
and start again, caught between fiendish

commands to cast me down to the damp
pit yawning underneath me and seraphic

insinuations to raise me up to their pillows
of humid spice, welcome my shattered mind
back to their clouds of diminished light.

HONEY ON MY TONGUE

Being the perfect witness and being honest
are seldom the same thing when testimony
isn't under oath and the outcome's already
pre-determined if not destined, but I was still
too young to understand how sweet lies are
for some, so I sat down first for the informal
manager's test and told the truth when asked
what drugs I tried, too many Yeses from
those self-medicating nights and long days

of frying and lifting and scrubbing and
pouring out blood and sweat for minimum-
wage-or-slightly-better paychecks that
often went back to buy the best medication
I could find on my carousel stuck endlessly
spinning if I didn't understand at seventeen
how to step off, thought changing uniforms
would be a brass ring rather than a tighter
collar around my neck, a black string tie

the next link in a chain that wasn't gold
like the Colonel's original for his pocket-
watch, but instead bone and gristle, either
mine or other boys or women or men
I would enlist like I had signed on nearly
three years before. I didn't know better
than to think the interview a success until
my manager took me aside the next day,
told me I had two perfect scores out of

three categories, but one hundred percent
on Honesty isn't the best thing when
eighty-five or ninety would do, he said.
I knew what he meant then, so I went back
to work since there were still hours to be
filled and chickens, always more chickens
to be fried to a crisp golden brown. I did
begin to notice how this latest manager's
hands lingered on the shoulders of the girls

I worked with at night, the women who
labored the day shifts when I came in
at three, out early from my senior-year
classes so I could get two more hours in
each time I worked. I can't say I watched
my co-workers from the sink or fryer or
breading station because I was concerned
at first—I was a seventeen-year-old boy
still watching women and girls the way

a seventeen-year-old boy will do—but I
did notice the women would try to move
to find space where he'd left none, one girl
would disappear into the Ladies room,
not coming out until another was sent in
to retrieve her or the manager would go
and knock on the door, threaten to punch
her out on the time clock and send her home.
When one of the women asked if I would

go with her on my day off with that same
girl and meet with the district manager
and one of the franchise owners, tell them
what I'd seen, I agreed and went back to
the office I had failed my first test sure
of success this time, sure that honest words
should be sweet and sustaining, pure as honey
on the tongue when spoken with conviction
that truth is stronger than lies, but when I

arrived the woman and the girl had already
come and gone, fired for stirring up trouble.
As I sat with those two men and my manager,
they all said what a bright future I had ahead
of me with them, how I could take my test
a second time and they were sure the results
would be much better, that I had learned
a lot since then. Of course, they were right.
But they didn't understand when I quit.

CODA

Through a freak of history, Harland Sanders bridged the cultural history of three centuries of American striving; he personifies it in some special, unrepeatable way. There can never be another like him.

—Josh Ozersky, *Colonel Sanders and the American Dream*

THE KING IS DEAD

Harland David Sanders (September 9, 1890 – December 16, 1980)

I resigned from the Colonel's army just weeks before
its General lay still in Louisville, reclining in ruffled
satin pillowing about him like the black crêpe paper
circling the portrait hanging in over six thousand stores

in forty-eight countries. A coffin photograph that looked
more 1880 than 1980 emerged as the last frozen image
of the decidedly 20th century man, who transformed himself
from railroad man, failed lawyer, motel owner to kindly cook

for a hungry hurried nation, but he sold himself short
twice over to savvier corporate faces who learned they
couldn't buy stubbornness and spite on the cheap. I knew
that feeling of being cheated, but my debt wouldn't sort

out in greasy silver slipping from my fingers, paper money
not fit to wipe away the years of grime and cosmic slop.
Other men owned that blame, not a face on a striped bucket
that would spill out its fill of golden crisp vice, sweetness

in the air like butter melting over the idea of home cooking
and family gathering for forgotten prayer led by the South's
only true Santa, trading the red suit and the early true black
for the ice-cream promise of a friendly plantation, looking

on the never-was past as America fell back in love, a crush
on its most unfaithful and embarrassing region, a bad
child who never fails to remind the rest of the country
she's only family when she wants, but her humid lush

lips offer the sweetest pucker, the rich deep flavors to die
for—and many have. From the side of the dark highway
in Corbin, Kentucky, where after changing tires and cleaning
motel rooms day and night and day, he still found time

to try recipe upon almost-right recipe until some alchemical
flavor was good enough to make Social Security a distant
future, to become the face children would recognize before
any President. It's too bad he would still hate the food.

Animated and Extra Crispy™

"...less of course Colonel get funky"
echoes from beyond the grave to shill
Popcorn Chicken™, "mouth poppin' good"
though it reminds you of the actual old
man calling the Extra Crispy™ "a damn
fried doughball stuck on some chicken,"
and a Spicy Tender Roast Sandwich™
he wouldn't recognize or choke down,
even if it's covered in Monterey Jack
cheese and meant to keep "the burger
boys" at bay. The cloying Honey BBQ
Wings™ might cause a "buzz" among
yellow jackets, but no one else should
want to be "stricken" with a "zingy"
sauce or anything else, chicken pot pie
and no-bone crispy strips aside this wasn't
a mascot to pitch Triple Crunch™ or
any other fancy sandwich but a flesh-
and-blood founder who died thinking
the corporate gravy "ain't fit for my dogs"
or anybody else's either, who would have
taken his cane, or the pressure cooker
he carried from small town or big city
and beaten George Hamilton with it
until the tanned Extra Crispy™ Colonel
was black and blue, bruised all over
with the disdain that a mere nickel with
every chicken could never draw or erase.

The Claudia Sanders Dinner House

CORBIN, KY.   Sanders Court and Cafe

41—Jct, with 25, 25 E. 1/2 Mi. N. of Corbin
Open all year except Xmas
A very good place to stop en route to Cumberland Fall
and the Great Smokies. Continuous 24-hour service.
Sizzling steaks, fried chicken, country ham, hot biscuits.
L., 50c to $1; D., 60c to $1.

—Adventures in Good Eating:
A Duncan Hines Book,
Good Eating Places Along
the Highways of America (1939)

I went to his last restaurant first,
the portraits of Kentucky Derby
winners and holiday wreaths lining
the walls of the warm rooms, cozy
like a home-cooked meal, which
was what this place promised when,
disgusted by gravy he said tasted
like "wallpaper paste" and corporate
bosses he knew didn't care what
an ornery old man had to say about
anything, he decided to show them
one last time how things should be
done, opened The Colonel's Lady
Dinner House featuring Original
Recipe™ though he long ago sold
the exclusive right to that product,
the right to his image and his name,
and when the company ever-so-gently
reminded him of that, he sued them
for over a hundred million dollars
before settling for one million and

the right to run the restaurant not far
from corporate headquarters, only
forced to change the name to his wife's.

A far cry from "Hell's Half-Acre" and
Corbin, Kentucky. Those hills still
poor today, in 1929, he had to fight
for everything, gunplay even to win
a gas station war that left two dead,
and in this sundown town on U.S. 25
he realized there weren't many places
to eat around here so he fed the drivers
until the Sanders Service Station
became the Sanders Service Station
and Cafe and then the Sanders Cafe
and Service Station and finally
the Sanders Court and Cafe, where
he built a model room, full size, inside
the middle of the dining room so he
could convince tired travelers to stay.

Close to the site of the original,
a store serves both as a museum and
a working franchise location, a place
I could buy today's products and then
sit down in the past, wooden chairs
and tables across from the glass cases
and shining counter, the replica motel
room built again in the middle, though
the motor court was long gone. So was
the Colonel, no longer around to tell
railroad stories in colorful language,
to entertain guests with the antics
of his pet bird, Jim Crow, that picked
shiny pennies out of his shirt, and I

think about that other Jim Crow, know
that no matter what he wanted to do
Harland Sanders would have known
to serve everyone equally in his time
would have meant neighbors coming
in the night to burn him out. Sometimes
history has no answers, but I wonder
if this man, who seemed to like most
people except those who wouldn't
follow directions and lawyers, met
travelers he couldn't serve in the front
room in the back, his love of feeding
the hungry and his love for money
coming together in those early days
like they would at the end for him.

When I sat down at the Dinner House,
the only thing dividing those patrons
was Red and Blue, Louisville Cardinal
fan or Big Blue Nation, and I ordered
my three-piece dinner, noticed the birds
were smaller, probably a local farm
supplying them fresh, and the chicken
was hot and tasty, the potatoes not
from a mix, and the gravy, oh the gravy
was a memory of flavor that I had
forgotten, must have taken care and, yes,
maybe even a little love, so I instinctively
bowed my head, not in prayer, perhaps,
but at least in gratitude, to give thanks.

Works Cited

"Julia Child." An Interview by Polly Frost. Appearing in *Interview Magazine: The Crystal Ball of Pop* on July 16, 2009.

A portion of the text from the back cover of the album *Colonel Sanders' Tijuana Picnic*. Mark56 Records, 1968.

Psalm 118:24, King James Version (KJV), The Bible

Farlex Partner Medical Dictionary. S.v. "full-thickness burn." Retrieved from https://medical-dictionary.thefreedictionary.com/full-thickness+burn

Upton Sinclair. *The Jungle* (unabridged edition from the 1906 original). Dover Publications, 2001.

The quote from Duncan Hines is originally from *Adventures in Good Eating: A Duncan Hines Book ; Good Eating Places along the Highways of America*, 1939. Taken from an image of the original guidebook.

I owe much of my research to the facts of the life of Colonel Harland Sanders to two sources:

Col. Harland Sanders. *Life as I Have Known It Has Been "Finger Lickin' Good."* Creation House; Carol Stream, IL, 1974.

Josh Ozersky. *Colonel Sanders and the American Dream.* University of Texas Press; Austin, TX, 2012.

ABOUT THE AUTHOR

Jon Tribble is author of
two collections of poems:
Natural State (Glass Lyre
Press, 2016) & *And There
Is Many a Good Thing*
(Salmon Poetry, 2017).
His poems have appeared
in print journals and
anthologies, including
*Ploughshares, Poetry,
Crazyhorse, Quarterly
West,* and *The Jazz Poetry
Anthology,* and online
at *The Account, Prime
Number,* and *storySouth.*
A group of his poems
was selected as the 2001
winner of the Campbell
Corner Poetry Prize from
Sarah Lawrence College.
He is the recipient of a
2003 Artist Fellowship
Award in Poetry from the
Illinois Arts Council and
is managing editor of *Crab Orchard Review* and series editor of the Crab
Orchard Series in Poetry published by SIU Press.

Glass Lyre Press

exceptional works to replenish the spirit

Glass Lyre Press is an independent literary publisher interested in technically accomplished, stylistically distinct, and original work. Glass Lyre seeks diverse writers that possess a dynamic aesthetic and an ability to emotionally and intellectually engage a wide audience of readers.

Glass Lyre's vision is to connect the world through language and art. We hope to expand the scope of poetry and short fiction for the general reader through exceptionally well-written books, which evoke emotion, provide insight, and resonate with the human spirit.

Poetry Collections
Poetry Chapbooks
Select Short & Flash Fiction
Anthologies

www.GlassLyrePress.com

CPSIA information can be obtained
at www.ICGtesting.com
Printed in the USA
LVHW100621180123
737337LV00004B/751

9 781941 783450